T0199185

Personal Financial Stewardship (Companion Workbook)

The Step-by-Step Guide to Debt-Free Living

CHRISTOPHER HOLMES

Copyright © 2019 Christopher Holmes.

All rights reserved. No part of this book may be used or reproduced by any means, graphic, electronic, or mechanical, including photocopying, recording, taping or by any information storage retrieval system without the written permission of the author except in the case of brief quotations embodied in critical articles and reviews.

WestBow Press books may be ordered through booksellers or by contacting:

WestBow Press
A Division of Thomas Nelson & Zondervan
1663 Liberty Drive
Bloomington, IN 47403
www.westbowpress.com
1 (866) 928-1240

Because of the dynamic nature of the Internet, any web addresses or links contained in this book may have changed since publication and may no longer be valid. The views expressed in this work are solely those of the author and do not necessarily reflect the views of the publisher, and the publisher hereby disclaims any responsibility for them.

Any people depicted in stock imagery provided by Getty Images are models, and such images are being used for illustrative purposes only. Certain stock imagery © Getty Images.

Scripture taken from the NEW AMERICAN STANDARD BIBLE®, Copyright © 1960,1962,1963,1968,1971, 1972,1973,1975,1977,1995 by The Lockman Foundation. Used by permission. www.Lockman.org

ISBN: 978-1-9736-5555-8 (sc)
ISBN: 978-1-9736-5556-5 (e)

Print information available on the last page.

WestBow Press rev. date: 3/12/2019

Contents

Introduction

Congratulations on your purchase of this workbook, companion to the book titled, *Personal Financial Stewardship*, by Christopher Holmes. You will find this resource to be a very helpful guide separately or when used along with the book by the same name. This workbook was designed to be used as an individual study, as a resource for couples to study together, and as a group study guide.

The author developed this workbook to complement the book so readers will have an easier time conducting the important exercises. This resource will focus more on the worksheets associated with developing your spending plans and other related action steps. There is even an expanded section on the "rapid debt reduction strategy." You have made a huge step toward a healthier financial future.

If you are the leader of a group discussion, this tool will help you to facilitate a class each week depending upon how your class is structured. This work book also makes a great guide for a marriage enrichment program or a pre-marital course, knowing money is such an important dynamic within any relationship. Be sure to fully engage in the exercises. They will be your guide toward a healthier, debt-free future. Enjoy your journey becoming a stronger financial steward.

PART A (Your Spending Plan)

Welcome to the beginning of your stewardship journey. Congratulations on your decision to start having a healthier relationship with your finances. The time you spend on this material, and the time you invest in doing the exercises, can make all the difference in your life.

Before digging into what is arguably the most important aspect of good stewardship—a well thought out spending plan, let's first start by understanding some equally important concepts about being a good money manager. *C. Holmes*

Why Get Your Finances in Order?

Picture going up to the airport ticket counter and asking the attendant for a ticket. The first thing they will ask you is where you want to go. Would you tell them it does not matter—that anywhere will do? Sounds strange, right? This is how some people view their lives and how they approach their financial futures. If it doesn't matter where you end up then it does not matter what you do in the meantime with your money. But if you do care where you end up, you will want to first establish where you want to go and why.

Are you tired of having too much month left at the end of the money? Are you worried about how you are going to send your kids through college? Are you concerned about having anything when you retire? Or perhaps, you are just tired of the creditors bothering you about paying your bills. Your motivation may be something you want to achieve in your life. Perhaps you feel passionate about doing some missions work. Without something to excite you about the work it will take to manage a healthy money management routine, chances are you may not follow through. It is a little like a diet. You must have a good reason to want to lose weight and stick to the plan or you may get discouraged.

If your doctor said that you needed to go on a diet, how would that make you feel? Perhaps not too good. But if the doctor said she is putting you on an eating plan, you may not mind that. It is the same with a budget. You are really developing a *spending plan* and not something that appears like hand cuffs for your life. Although, at first, a budget may feel a bit like hand cuffs. After a while the spending plan you embrace in this workbook will begin to bear fruit and you will be encouraged to keep following the plan. Follow the step-by-step instructions. You will begin to see a real difference in your life within a few months.

Note: See section F for the answers to the questions within this workbook.

Question 1 – How would you describe the things you have been doing to prevent yourself from experiencing a healthier financial situation?

_____

_____

Question 2 – What is the most important reason you have for getting your finances in order?

_____

_____

Your Spending Plan

The first thing to get a strong handle on is your own spending plan. You may have been keeping a budget in your head which is better than nothing. But, it is not even close to ideal. It is essential you take the time to create a record of your current financial habits using _Form A_ below. You will later be guided through other exercises designed to help you identify what steps to take for a progressively healthier plan for financial blessings.

Note: Be sure to convert all the figures you enter as a monthly figure.

Begin by filling in the numbers associated with each sub-category in Form A. For example, under the housing category, enter your monthly mortgage or rent. Then, enter what you pay monthly for electricity, oil, gas, etc. If you pay any of these within a period other than monthly, be sure to convert all the figures to a monthly amount. If you pay your trash quarterly, take a third of that amount and enter it. Same for your car insurance. If you pay that every six months, place one sixth of that amount in the field. If you happen to pay something twice per month, then double it do make a monthly number. This is especially important for the areas like groceries, gasoline and miscellaneous. You can refer to the companion book for an explanation as to why this is so important.

Note: Be sure not to double any of your expenses by accident. Listing your _net-spendable income_ helps to prevent this error. Perhaps your employer automatically takes out your car payment and your health insurance for example. If you used your gross (pre-deduction) income in the worksheet below, you could be calculating those auto-withdrawals twice by accident.

Question 3 – The Biblical concept of you being the manager of the things God lets you use while you are here on earth is known as what? How would you explain this in your own words?

_____

_____

Question 4 – Complete this scriptural statement from Matthew 6:21; For where your _____ is, there your heart will be also. Can you give an everyday example of this concept?

_____

_____

Form A (Spending Plan Form)

A.	**Housing Total:**			**F.**	**Miscellaneous:**			
	Mortgage/rent				Subscriptions			
	Electricity				Coffee/drinks			
	Oil				Snacks			
	Gas				Makeup/nails			
	Water				Hair style/cuts			
	Sewer				Dry cleaning			
	Trash				Lunches			
	Insurance				Gifts			
	Taxes				Cash			
	Maintenance				other			
	Cell phone			**G.**	**Clothing:**			
B.	**Auto Total:**				Shoes			
	Payments				Outfits			
	Fuel				Coats			
	Insurance				other			
	Maintenance			**H.**	**School:**			
	Other				Materials			
C.	**Insurances:**				Day care			
	Medical				Tuition			
	Life				other			
	Identity			**I.**	**Groceries:**			
	other				Food, etc.			
D.	**Entertainment:**			**J.**	**Debt Totals:**			
	Dining				Personal Loans			
	Take out				Credit cards			
	Day trips				School loans			
	Vacations			**K.**	**Savings:**			
	Movies			**L.**	**Investments:**			
	Hobbies			**M.**	**Giving/tithing**			
	Baby sitting							
	Internet/TV				**Total Expenses:**			
	other				**Income:**			
E.	**Health:**							
	Medication				**Difference (+/-)**			
	Dentist							
	Doctor							
	other				**Be sure to convert all figures to a monthly amount.**			

See worksheet B for further guidance on your loans and credit card debts.

After you have entered all the required fields, you are ready to do the math. For each main category add up the associated sub-categories for a total category number. Repeat this for every main category. Then add up all the main categories for a total expense number at the bottom. Finally, subtract the total expense number from your total income. Take your time with this part of the exercise. Double check your math with a calculator if needed. You want to be as close as possible without worrying about it being to the exact dollar. Once completed, you will see the bottom line—the number which may be causing you the trouble! Of course this is referring to the number in the "difference" field at the end. If this number is positive, or your monthly income is larger than your total expenses, then you can pat yourself on the back for being a good steward.

If, however, your "difference" number is negative, or your total expense number is higher than your total income number per month, then you have some more work to do (and some more stewardship principles to adopt). Even if your expenses are lower than your monthly income, you still may need to make some improvements in order to move your finances to a higher level. Remember, a balanced budget is really just the first step in becoming free from debt.

Question 5 – How would you make this inaccurate statement true? "Money is the root of all evil."

_____

_____

Question 6 – Why is the love of money so dangerous as warned in I Timothy 6:10?

_____

_____

PART B (Consumer Debt Listing)

Use *Form B* to help you identify your monthly credit card obligations to be entered in the spending plan (Form A). Form B will also be used to assist you in the "rapid-debt-reduction" later in this workbook.

Note: You will NOT be listing your mortgage, rent, or auto payments into this form. Form B is designed to help manage your consumer debts like personal loans, credit card bills, medical bills, and even school loans.

Form B (Debt Listings Form)

Important: Be sure to list your consumer debts in order from the largest balances to the smallest:

Largest to smallest debt balances:	Owed to:	Minimum payment:	Comment:
Example: $8,000	ABC Credit Card	$85.00	Paying minimum
Example: $6,000	XYZ College	$145.00	Payments on hold
1.			
2.			
3.			
4.			
5.			
6.			
7.			
8.			
9.			
10.			
11.			
12.			
Total Debt: $	Total Monthly:	$	

After you have entered all you consumer debts, add up columns one and three. The first column will show you the total consumer debt burden you have on your shoulders. The third column will show your monthly consumer debt burden. Whether you are paying your school loan currently or not, be sure to add it up in the total. Planning to pay early on a school loans is good stewardship.

Question 7 – Why are patience and delayed gratification so important in the establishment of a balanced spending plan?

_____

_____

Question 8 – Since borrowing is not a sin, what part of the borrowing process can get us into trouble, or be considered sinful? (See Psalm 37:21 for a clue).

_____

_____

PART C (Budget Analysis)

Use this spending plan analysis form (*Form C*) to help you see where you may need to make some changes to your spending habits. It can also be used to help you develop a revised spending plan. You can design it to balance your budget and align it toward freedom from consumer debt. More on this later.

Go ahead and take the numbers you have in the *totals* fields for each main budget category and write them in the column labelled "Current."

Note that the "Compare" column is completed by using Form D in the next section. Use it to establish the guideline percentage per main category. See section D on page 23 at this point for further details.

Question 9 – Since God promises to provide for our needs, we as good stewards must heed what caution regarding our wants or desires? (See Proverbs 16:18).

_____

_____

Question 10 – God tends to answer our prayers with yes, no, or not now. Where in your financial future should you be okay with getting the answer "not now?"

_____

_____

Question 11 – What have you been doing to "keep up with the Jones" that you will no longer be doing with God's help?

_____

_____

Form C (Analysis worksheet)

Category:	Current:	Compare:	Difference:	Change?	Projection:
A. Housing					
B. Automobile					
C. Insurances					
D. Entertainment					
E. Health					
F. Miscellaneous					
G. Clothing					
H. School					
I. Groceries					
J. Debts					
K. Savings					
L. Investments					
M. Giving/tithing					
N. Totals...					
Comments:					

Completing the Compare Column

Look at the housing category as the first example. Suppose your net spendable income is $45,000 annually. Now, look at Chart D below for the percentage where the housing row intersects the $45,000 column to find 34%. You may find it easier to use the calculator feature on your mobile device for this section. Now enter a twelfth of $45,000 or 3,750 into your calculator. Then, multiply it by 0.34 (34%) to get $1,275 as the guideline amount for your budget.

You are taking a twelfth of your annual income because we are working with monthly figures. You multiply that twelfth ($3,750) by 34% because that is the guideline percentage in this case (from Chart D). You ended up with $1,275 as the recommended amount for your housing category in this example. Your actual numbers will differ of course. Be sure to follow the chart and this basic formula to get your correct numbers in the Compare column.

This second example will help you further see exactly what needs to be done for all of the main categories down the Compare column. Take another look at Chart D for where the automobile row intersects with $45,000 to find 12%. Now take a month's worth of your net income or $3,750 and multiply it by 0.12 (12 %) to get $450, which is the guideline amount for your automobile comparison column.

Get it now? You can now go through all your other categories using your actual numbers and do the same math until you have a number in each field down the whole Compare column. Take your time with this section too.

By now you should have columns Current and Compare filled in. Next is to subtract the numbers from each row to get the differences per row. Look again at the housing row. You may have a number in the field called "Current" something like $2,150 and $1,275 in the field called "Compare" for housing. Subtract them to get $850 in this example.

Likewise for the automobile category. Take the *Current* number which may be $650 and the *Compare* number in this example is $450. So that difference is $200 to be entered in the *Difference* column. You should be able to follow the same process to determine the differences for each pair down the columns for your actual budget numbers.

Question 12 – Why is hoarding a bad idea? What is a better way to approach savings? (*Refer to the companion book for more details*).

_____

_____

Question 13 – What would you say is the greatest enemy of being a good steward? (See Luke 12:15 for a hint).

_____

_____

Do You Need to Make Any Changes?

The first part of this "Change" section is easy. You only need to write yes or no in each field of the *Change* column in *Form C*. Where your number in the *Current* field is smaller than the Compare number, you can write a *no* in the Change column because that means you are living within the budget guideline for that category. Likewise, where you have a Current number larger than the Compare number, place a *yes* in that associated Change field. This means you may have some corrective actions to consider for that category. More on this shortly.

Now, take a closer look at the Change column as it relates to the Projection column. This may require you to go back and take a closer inspection of your budget sub-categories on Form A. At this point you can ignore the categories which have a "no" in them. This means you do not have to develop an action plan for change in that category. You can focus on the typical three or four categories people tend to have a "yes." This means you may have to come up with one or more corrective action plans for every category containing a yes in the Change column. A yes means those categories appear to be over the budget guideline as compared to section D.

It may appear over budget because, in some cases, there is a very good reason for a particular main category to be too high. For example, you may not have any school or vacation expenses which can compensate for what may appear to be a high housing category. But, do not use that as a cop-out. You may still need to dig deep and determine if you can truly cut back in one or more of the sub-categories in order to bring that budget item into better alignment. You will need to determine a target number for the last column (Projection) in order to better align it with your spending plan over the next six months.

Note that in the categories where there is a legitimate reason for it being high (such as housing, health, or school), you may have noticed it is okay if you are below budget in one or two other areas. Those lower spending areas are essentially allowing you to afford the over spending in the other areas.

Question 14 – Can you match the items? Below are typical examples of short, medium, and long range personal finance goals. Identifying them as short, medium, or long range goals:

_____ - Deciding how to pack for your trip to Hawaii.
_____ - Deciding how to cut $50 out of your clothing spending category.
_____ - Sitting down with your spouse next year to evaluate your budget progress.
_____ - Calling creditors to see if you can get your interest or payments reduced.
_____ - Sitting with an investment broker about where to put your extra savings.

Part C should cause you to stretch outside your comfort zone. It may also cause you to consider some sacrificial actions as necessary. This is perhaps the hardest part of the financial self-examination. Moreover, it can be the most impactful if done sincerely. No pain no gain, as the saying goes. After you make the necessary changes (and sacrifices) to your future spending habits, it will allow you to do so many more exciting things. The pain associated with the initial financial examination will be long forgotten by the time you are reaping the rewards of being a good steward.

It may be at this point you go back and remind yourself why you want to be debt-free. Even though the exercises may be completed, this is really just the beginning with regard to actually putting your action plans into place over the next many months, or perhaps even years in some extreme budget alignment situations.

Question 15 – What does it mean in Proverbs 13:7 that acting rich will make you poor, and acting poor will make you rich?

_____
_____

Question 16 – With regard to your budgeting practices, what does this saying mean, "What gets measured gets managed?"

_____
_____

Your family situation may be different. But, for this example, suppose you have three categories which are over the recommended guideline (the ones with a *yes* in the change column): activities, miscellaneous, and groceries for example. In this case it is necessary to come up with specific action plans lowering these three categories within a six month period or so.

In the activities area for example, you could decide to eat out every-other week instead of every week. You could meet with your church family for lunch once per month rather than every Sunday. You can rent movies rather than going to the theater every time. You get the idea. What habits can you revise so the activities (in your Change categories) align with the guideline amount over the next six months or so?

After brainstorming, you can do the math to calculate what expenses those actions will eliminate from each category. Then, place that new total in the Projection column as your reduction target. For example, if you decided you need to change two habits to reduce your monthly expenses in your activities category, and those two habits reduce your monthly expenses by an estimated $35 and $15, you can place your original Current figure *minus* the $50 you are projecting to reduce. Place that new number in the associated Projection column. You are basically setting a new, lower target number to strive for over the next six months' worth of habit changes. Do this for each row containing a "yes" to establish your total goals for improved financial habits.

Same thing with the Miscellaneous expenses for example. What habits can be changed to bring this category into alignment? Can you buy coffee on the way to work once per week and make your coffee at home the rest of the week? Can you pack a snack rather than buying one from the vending machine? Can you go out for lunch only once or twice per week and pack your lunch the other days? These suggestions could easily cut $100 to $200 out of this spending category monthly. You can think of even more ideas. Estimate those monthly savings and write that revised, lower number in the Projected column.

Question 17 – List some cost reduction actions you can take, regardless of whether a particular budget category is too high or not?

_____

_____

Finally in this example, what are some habit changes that can be made to reduce your Groceries category? Perhaps you can start planning your weekly meals around what is on sale rather than going to the store daily to see what you are in the mood to eat. You could start using coupons. You can make sure you are not hungry when you go food shopping. Examine what else you can change to positively impact this budget category needed.

The categories you may need to take a hard look at will be different. Still, you can apply the same brainstorming exercise to it. Sometimes it helps to challenge yourself with one or two others who know you well, and care about your success with this improvement journey. Praying for guidance can help a great deal too. Also, keep in mind the sacrifices you put in place are not meant to be permanent. It may be for the first six month period or one year for example. At the point where your overall spending plan begins to look sound, you can consider going back to those original habits because you should be able to afford them by then.

Continue the *Form C, Projection* exercise until you believe you have exhausted all the possible ways you can reduce your expenses for the categories which were over the recommended guideline (Chart D). This will be your first six month plan. The goal is to consistently free up some seed money so you can apply it to your consumer debts. This is explained in the "rapid debt reduction strategy" starting on page 26.

PART D (Spending Guide)

This Form D guide is to be used in conjunction with the the analysis Form C. Keep in mind this is only a guide and should not be considered specific advice. These guidelines are offered to assist you in determining whether your expenses are within reason per budget category, versus being too far out of range. Even still, there may be reasons to be outside the ranges in either direction. Again, use it as a *guide* relative to your spending plans. You can read more on this topic in the companion book, *Personal Financial Stewardship*.

Question 18 – Why does the Bible suggest we are to learn from the ant with regard to our financial resources? (see Proverbs 6:6-8).

_____

_____

Question 19 – Are you including prayer when you are deciding how to redesign your budget and goals? Proverbs 3:6 says, "In all your ways acknowledge Him, and He will make your paths straight." Write your prayer for you path here:

_____

_____

Question 20 – Instead of striving to be the richest person in the cemetery, what are some other noble causes you could support along the way? What dream of yours does this stimulate?

_____

_____

Form D (Guide for Category Percentages)

Net Income	$25,000	$35,000	$45,000	$65,000	$75,000	$85,000
A. Housing	38%	36%	34%	30%	29%	28%
B. Automobile	13%	13%	12%	11%	10%	9%
C. Insurance	5%	5%	5%	5%	5%	5%
D. Entertainment	4%	5%	5%	6%	7%	7%
E. Health	5%	4%	4%	4%	4%	4%
F. Miscellaneous	4%	5%	5%	6%	8%	8%
G. Clothing	3%	4%	4%	5%	5%	5%
H. School	5%	5%	4%	3%	3%	3%
I. Groceries	6%	5%	5%	5%	4%	4%
J. Debts	5%	5%	5%	5%	5%	5%
K. Savings	2%	3%	4%	5%	5%	5%
L. Investments	N/A	N/A	3%	5%	5%	7%
M. Giving/tithing	10%	10%	10%	10%	10%	10%

Adapted from the Percentage Guide for Family Income form, Christian Financial Concepts, Inc. 1996. [1]

Other than this chart being a guide only, take a closer look at some of its elements. Perhaps the most obvious aspect is that the less income one has, the higher the percentage needs to be spent on the housing, automobile, and grocery categories. With a lower income, it becomes a greater struggle to align categories such as debts, savings, investments, and giving as well. You may have noticed the income section is not always a match. If your income is not an exact match on one of these columns, simply go with the column closest to your income on Chart D. For example, if your net income is $51,000, then go with the column of percentages under the field labeled "$45,000." If your net income is over $85,000, just use the percentages under the column labeled "$85,000" as your guide.

You will notice there is no percentage listed in some of the investment fields on Chart D. This is because initially, at least, you may need to delay investing until enough progress has been made with your corrective action efforts. Those farther along in the stewardship process should be investing near the listed guidelines as shown in Chart D.

Question 21 – Proverbs 13:18 warns that poverty and shame will come to those who neglect discipline. What areas of your financial stewardship journey may require you to exercise more discipline?

_____

_____

Question 22 – Indulgences are ok as long as they are part of your what?

_____

_____

Question 23 – What numbers (1-4) need to be in front of these steps to place them in order for healthy financial managing?

___ Start investing at least 10% of your earnings.
___ Start saving enough every month in order to carve out money for debt reduction.
___ Complete a spending plan form showing your current spending habits.
___ Balance your budget.

Question 24 – Describe the corrective action steps you are planning to put in place over the next six months:

_____

_____

Rapid Debt Reduction Strategy (Back to Form B)

In the companion book, there is a part where Chris Holmes describes a non-conventional method for getting rid of your consumer debts relatively fast. It is at least faster than if you took the path of debt consolidation. Consolidation of your debts is not a bad thing. It is certainly better than doing nothing. However, there is a better way to rid yourself of your consumer debt burdens, and perhaps you will even get excited about the process.

Take a look at your completed Form B with all your consumer debts listed. These are the ones which are hurting your current budget, and the ones which would hold back your future financial goals if you did not eliminate them. Here is where you learn the reason for listing the debts in order from highest balance to the lowest.

You did a lot of work earlier to identify where you can cut back in your higher spending plan categories. As a result, you should have been able to calculate an overall savings reduction in the Projection column of Form C. Assume you were able to identify $200 in total projected savings every month starting with your third month. Perhaps, you projected as much as $350 per month will be available after sixth months. Your actual numbers will vary.

In this example, once you reach the third month of your plan, you should have the extra $200 available to put against your debts on Form B. Here's how. Start with the lowest balance first (or the one at the bottom of your list). It could be a $1,500 balance for your dentist or it could be $800 you owe to your brother. Use the extra $200 to pay off the lowest balance, no matter what the interest rates are for the other debts. As a result, you can have the dentist debt paid in full within eight months in this example. You can have your brother paid back in only four months.

If you were paying the dentist $50 per month, you can add that to the available $350 you have six months later for a total of $400 to pay toward those debts monthly. Now, suppose the next lowest balance you owe to the credit card company is $4,000. You will want to take the now available $400 and add that to the regular monthly payment of $75 in this example. By placing the $475 on that bill every month, you will have it paid off in only nine months instead of the five years or more it would have taken paying just the minimum monthly.

Think of this process as *compounding your payments*. Rather than spending the freed up funds, you keep taking the paid off amounts and adding them together for a larger amount to apply to the next largest debt until they are all paid off.

Continuing with the example, you would take the available $475 along with the next minimum payment which could be $100 added together for a new total of $500 you can put toward the next pay off balance. This tends to be a more effective method of paying off debts for a couple reasons. One, it is a faster way to pay off your debts than consolidating them for a lower monthly payment. Second, you are less likely to get discouraged about your overall debt improvement efforts as a result of seeing the big impact you can make relatively fast.

If you take a big marker and draw a thick line through the debt line on Form B each time you pay off a balance, how is that going to make you feel? Excited, right? You can keep crossing out those debts one line at a time and high-five someone.

Question 25 – How can you get your finances to the point where you are *earning* interest rather than *paying* (usually higher) interest every month?

_____

_____

This would still not be the end of your stewardship journey. After your consumer debts are paid off and you have hundreds of dollars left over at the end of each month, you still need to do one more step. It is an enjoyable one, thankfully. Start learning how to *invest* your money for future spending like the mission trips you want to support, sending your children to college, that dream vacation, retirement, or helping to put an education wing on your church, etc.

Remember that it all starts with carving out a little seed money from your spending habit changes to be used to pay down your debts. Then you can use those savings to cover emergencies such your refrigerator or lawn mower dying. That might be a buffer of $3,000 or so. Anything over that you should take from savings and invest it. You can see the "celebrating milestones chart" section in the companion book for more general guidance. There are plenty of good investment agents and insurance agents with whom you can consult when the time comes to invest. That will be a great problem to have and a definite stewardship milestone—having money left at the end of the month!

Question 26 – Explain the basic difference between spending money and investing money in your own words.

_____

_____

PART E (Stewardship)

Part E does not have a form associated with it. However, it encompasses some other general direction also found in the companion book, *Personal Financial Stewardship*.

Have You Committed to Giving?

One of the areas some clients are tempted to stop doing while they get their finances in order is to stop tithing at church, or to stop giving to other humanitarian causes. As tempting as this may seem, it would not be a good idea. It may sound counter-intuitive to tithe or give to causes when they really do not have the rest of their finances in order. I thought the same thing when I started down this path. I was fortunate to be challenged to still give on faith and see how God blessed me.

Giving to God is not the same as giving to a bank and expecting a financial return. In some cases God will bless you with money. Sometimes He blesses your faithfulness with help from others (making it seems like a miracle). Your child may qualify for a competitive college grant or scholarship. Your car may go years beyond what you expected it to go and still be safe. Your health may be improved, or you may get a promotion. These are just examples. God can do these things and so much more. Give to God. Don't wait to test Him on this. See what floodgates He opens in your life. Jumping directly into giving ten percent back to God is the best approach. If you feel strongly that you need to start smaller and then step-up to ten percent or more over time. God can honor this approach too, as long as you give with love in your heart.

Question 27 – In Malachi 3:10, what does God say He will do if you bring your first fruits (or tithe) into the storehouse?

_____

_____

Question 28 – Malachi 3:10 not only describes the benefit of tithing, it is also a time in the Bible where God says it's ok to _____ Him on this and see how He opens for floodgates for a _____.

Question 29 – In Malachi 3:8, it suggests we can rob God. How?

_____

_____

PART F (Answers to questions)

1. Self-determined answer/discussion.
2. Self-determined answer/discussion.
3. Stewardship. Plus self-determined answer/discussion.
4. Treasure. Plus self-determined answer/discussion.
5. The <u>love of money</u> is the root of all evil.
6. Brings many sorrows. Money must not be your god.
7. Helps you live within your means. Plus self-determined answer/discussion.
8. Not paying the debt back to the lender.
9. Pride. Lack of humility.
10. Perhaps investing or the family vacation. Self-determined answer/discussion.
11. Self-determined answer/discussion.
12. Hoarding is a sign of poor stewardship, selfishness, and a lack of faith. Savings accounts are for specific, future spending purposes.
13. Covetousness.
14. Long, short, medium, short, long.
15. A caution about over spending. Spiritual riches. Discussion.
16. Measuring is the way to manage progress. Discussion.
17. Self-determined answer/discussion.
18. Be self-disciplined and wise with your resources. Discussion.
19. Self-determined answer/discussion.
20. Tithing, missions work, supporting other non-profit organizations. Discussion.
21. Self-determined answer/discussion.
22. Balanced spending plan (or budget).
23. 4, 3, 1, 2.
24. Self-determined answer/discussion.
25. By following the steps outlined in question 23. Eliminating consumer debts. Discussion.
26. Investments can offer long term returns. Self-determined answer/discussion.
27. Open the floodgates of blessings.
28. Test. Blessing.
29. By not tithing and by withholding offerings.

Notes

1. Burkett, Larry. (1993). *Percentage Guide for Family Income (supplemental form).* Christian Financial Concepts, Inc.

About the Author

Christopher Holmes is the proprietor of his own professional training company. He has national experience as a contracted corporate trainer with *Fred Pryor Seminars,* and he has decades of experience as a certified personal finance and budget counselor through *Christian Financial Concepts, Inc.* In his earlier years, Chris worked as an operations manager for a large healthcare organization before entering the human resources field as a human resources consultant, later as a director of Human Resources.

Chris' wife, Renee, has been his business partner for a number of ventures. They ran a sales and marketing business through most of the 1990s, and they managed a real-estate investment business from 2010-2018. Most recently, he has launched into coaching others in business on why and how (step-by-step) to become debt-free. Chris is always excited to travel, to meet others, and to train those seeking the incredible power of stewardship principles in their personal finances.

When Chris is not training others, he can be found at home with his lovely family, reading self-improvement books of all kinds. In the warmer months, Chris and his family enjoy boating at the Chesapeake Bay or at lakes local to them in Pennsylvania. Renee and he raised three wonderful adult children. They can also be found on Sunday mornings worshipping at Bethany Church in Macungie, PA. For more information on his training offerings or to arrange for him to train within your organization, please contact him or his team at PFStewardship@gmail.com or on LinkedIn. Letters can be sent to P.O. Box 6, 33 South Home Avenue, Topton, PA 19562.

Printed in the United States
By Bookmasters